THE MORAL COMPASS CURRICULUM

A HOLISTIC APPROACH

DR. MINAKSHI BANSAL

DEDICATION

To the next generation, may you find your true north.

ᗡᗡᗡ

Contents

Contents

Prayer

"Om Bhadram Karnebhih Shrinuyama Devah

Bhadram Pashyemakshabhiryajatrah

Sthirairangais Tushtuvamsastanubhih

Vyashema Devahitam Yadayuh

Svasti Na Indro Vriddhashravah

Svasti Nah Pusha Vishwavedah

Svasti Nastarkshyo Arishtanemih

Svasti No Brihaspatir Dadhatu

Om Shantih Shantih Shantih"

This mantra is a prayer for universal well-being, invoking the blessings of various deities for protection, health, and happiness. It emphasizes the importance of experiencing the auspicious through all senses and living a life aligned with divine purpose. The repetition of "Shantih" at the end signifies a deep desire for peace in the individual, the environment, and the universe at large. This mantra is often recited as a prayer for peace, prosperity, and the physical and spiritual well-being of all beings.

ᐅᐅᐅ

About The Author

This book represents the culmination of extensive research and meticulous analysis, incorporating a diverse range of sources, including numerous books, scholarly studies, and personal experiences. Additionally, I have scoured various websites to gather relevant information and data essential for the compilation of this work. I have taken every precaution to ensure the accuracy of the information presented and have diligently cited all sources to acknowledge their contributions.

From her earliest days, Minakshi was distinguished by an insatiable appetite for reading. Her literary universe was inhabited by characters and narratives that spanned ethical tales, motivational and inspirational stories, and the mythic parables imbued with life lessons. This voracious reading habit was not merely for personal edification but was driven by a desire to distill and disseminate the essence of these narratives to foster the development of students and peers alike. She was particularly captivated by the lives and teachings of historical figures and spiritual leaders such as Adi Shankaracharya, Swami Vivekananda, Dr. APJ Abdul Kalam, Mahamana Pandit Madan Mohan Malviya, Mahatma Gandhi, Sardar Vallabhai Patel, and Vinoba Bhave, among others. Their philosophies and life stories fueled her ambition to embody their ideals of resilience, selflessness, and relentless pursuit of knowledge.

Dr. Minakshi's academic and practical engagement with psychology has been equally noteworthy. As a research scholar, her focus has been on exploring the intricate tapestry of the human psyche, aiming to unlock the potential for psychological well-being and societal harmony. Her scholarly work is complemented by her active involvement in social work, where she employs her academic insights to make tangible differences in the lives of the underprivileged. Her endeavours in social work are characterized by an innovative approach that combines traditional wisdom with contemporary psychological practices to address the multifaceted challenges faced by these communities.

Her artistic talents, another facet of her diverse capabilities, are not merely a personal passion but also serve as a medium through which she communicates and connects with others. Her art, rich in symbolism and emotional depth, reflects her philosophical inquiries and social concerns, offering viewers a glimpse into the breadth of her intellect and the depth of her compassion.

In addition to her contributions to the arts and social sciences, Dr. Minakshi has embraced the healing arts of Pranic Healing, mastering the techniques developed by Master Choa Kok Sui. This practice, which focuses on the manipulation of Prana or life energy to heal the body and aura, has been both a personal journey of discovery and a means through which she extends her healing touch to others. Her proficiency in Pranic Healing is complemented by her advocacy and teaching of various forms of meditation aimed at rejuvenation, personal betterment, and the cultivation of harmony within individuals and communities alike.

Dr. Minakshi's life is a narrative of relentless pursuit, not just of personal achievement but of the upliftment and empowerment of society at large. Her diverse interests and talents—spanning the arts, literature, psychology, and the healing practices—converge on a singular path of service. She embodies the spirit of the luminaries who inspired her, channelling their legacy through her actions and teachings. Through her books, art, and social initiatives, she continues to inspire a new generation to embark on their own journeys of self-discovery, resilience, and altruism.

Her commitment to social betterment, particularly her focus on uplifting underprivileged children, reflects a deep understanding of the transformative potential of education and personal development. By integrating her knowledge of psychology, her artistic sensibilities, and her healing practices, Dr. Bansal has developed a holistic approach to social work that addresses both the immediate needs and the long-term well-being of the communities she serves.

As an author, Dr. Minakshi's writings offer a blend of inspirational insights, practical wisdom, and reflective contemplations drawn from her extensive reading and life experiences. Her books serve as a guide for those seeking to navigate the complexities of life with grace, resilience, and purpose. Through her narratives, she extends an invitation to her readers to explore the depths of their own potential and to contribute meaningfully to the collective well-being of society.

In Dr. Minakshi Bansal, we find a remarkable synthesis of the artist, the scholar, the healer, and the social activist. Her life's work stands as a beacon of hope and a source of inspiration for individuals seeking to make a difference in the world. Her story is a compelling reminder of the power of individual action, rooted in compassion and driven by a profound commitment to the betterment of humanity. Dr. Minakshi's legacy is not just in the tangible outcomes of her efforts but in the enduring spirit of inquiry, empathy, and service that she embodies.

ppp

Preface

In a world that whirls with dizzying speed, where technological advancements and societal shifts seem to outpace our capacity for ethical reflection, the need for a moral compass has never been more pressing. As an educator and lifelong advocate for character development, I have witnessed firsthand the profound impact that a strong moral foundation can have on individuals, communities, and society as a whole. It is with this conviction that I offer this curriculum, a holistic approach to cultivating the virtues and values that guide us toward a life of purpose, integrity, and compassion.

The seeds for this work were sown in the fertile ground of my own experiences as a student, teacher, and parent. I have witnessed the transformative power of education, not only in imparting knowledge and skills but also in shaping character and fostering ethical decision-making.

I have seen the hunger in young people for guidance and direction, for a framework that helps them navigate the complexities of life and make choices that align with their deepest values. And I have observed the profound impact that a lack of moral guidance can have, leading to confusion, disillusionment, and even despair.

This curriculum is not simply a collection of lessons or activities; it is a journey of self-discovery and moral growth. It is an invitation to explore the fundamental questions of human existence: What is right? What is good? How should we treat others?

What is our responsibility to the world around us? Through engaging stories, thought-provoking discussions, and practical exercises, this curriculum aims to equip learners with the tools they need to develop a strong moral compass, one that will guide them through life's challenges and lead them towards a life of purpose and meaning.

This approach is holistic in nature, recognizing that morality is not confined to a single domain or discipline. It encompasses our thoughts, feelings, actions, and relationships. It is woven into the fabric of our daily lives, influencing our choices, our interactions with others, and our contributions to society. This curriculum embraces this interconnectedness, weaving together insights from philosophy, psychology, literature, history, and other disciplines to create a rich and comprehensive tapestry of moral exploration.

The virtues and values explored in this curriculum are not new; they have been cherished by cultures and traditions throughout history. They include timeless principles such as honesty, integrity, compassion, respect, responsibility, fairness, courage, perseverance, gratitude, forgiveness, cooperation, self-discipline, humility, and generosity.

While these values may be expressed in different ways across cultures, their underlying essence remains the same: they are the qualities that enable us to live a life of purpose, meaning, and ethical integrity.

This curriculum is designed to be adaptable and flexible, catering to the diverse needs and interests of learners of all ages and backgrounds. It can be used in schools, community centers, religious institutions, or even in the home. The activities and exercises can be modified to suit different learning styles and levels of engagement.

The goal is not to impose a rigid set of rules or dogmas, but to foster critical thinking, open dialogue, and a deep appreciation for the complexity and nuance of moral decision-making.

It is my hope that this curriculum will inspire and empower

learners to embrace their own moral agency, to become active participants in shaping their lives and the world around them. I believe that by cultivating the virtues and values that lie at the heart of this curriculum, we can create a more just, compassionate, and sustainable world for ourselves and for generations to come.

Dr. Minakshi Bansal
Social Activist
Ahmedabad, Gujarat, Bharat

ONE

Introduction: The Importance of a Moral Compass

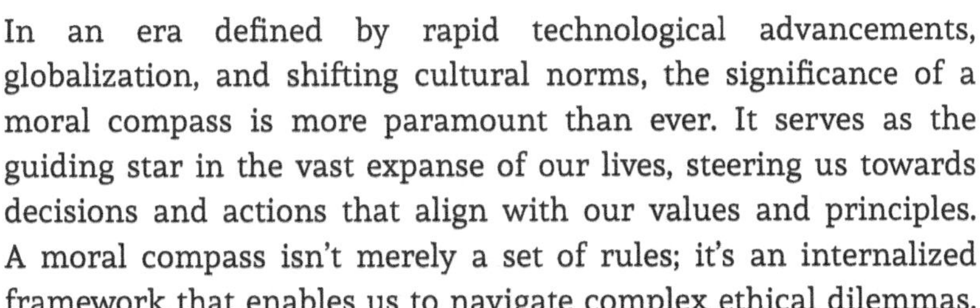

In an era defined by rapid technological advancements, globalization, and shifting cultural norms, the significance of a moral compass is more paramount than ever. It serves as the guiding star in the vast expanse of our lives, steering us towards decisions and actions that align with our values and principles. A moral compass isn't merely a set of rules; it's an internalized framework that enables us to navigate complex ethical dilemmas, forge meaningful relationships, and contribute positively to society.

At its core, a moral compass is the amalgamation of our beliefs, values, and ethical principles. It's the inner voice that prompts us to differentiate between right and wrong, good and bad, just and unjust. It's shaped by our upbringing, cultural background, personal experiences, and reflections on life's profound questions. While the components of a moral compass might vary among individuals and societies, its fundamental purpose remains the same: to guide us toward living a life of integrity and purpose.

The significance of a moral compass becomes evident when we consider its multifaceted impact on our lives. Firstly, it acts as a decision-making tool, aiding us in choosing the path that aligns with our values. In a world overflowing with information and choices, a moral compass provides a filter through which we can evaluate options and make sound judgments. It empowers us to act in accordance with our principles, even when faced with challenging situations where external pressures might tempt us to compromise.

Moreover, a moral compass fosters strong and meaningful relationships. When we consistently demonstrate honesty, integrity, and respect for others, we build trust and credibility. These qualities are essential for fostering healthy connections with friends, family, colleagues, and even strangers. A strong moral compass guides us to treat others with empathy and compassion, creating a foundation for harmonious interactions and mutual understanding.

In the broader context of society, a moral compass plays a crucial role in maintaining social order and promoting ethical behavior. When individuals adhere to a shared set of values, communities thrive. Trust flourishes, cooperation becomes the norm, and conflicts are resolved peacefully. A strong moral compass encourages individuals to act as responsible citizens, contributing to the well-being of their communities and upholding the principles upon which society is built.

The importance of a moral compass extends beyond our personal lives and interpersonal relationships. It also influences our professional endeavors. Ethical decision-making is a cornerstone of any successful organization. When employees possess a strong moral compass, they are more likely to act with integrity, uphold ethical standards, and prioritize the long-term success of the company over short-term gains. This not only builds a positive reputation for the organization but also contributes to a healthy and productive work environment.

In today's interconnected world, where information travels at lightning speed and actions have far-reaching consequences, a moral compass is more vital than ever. It helps us navigate the ethical challenges posed by technological advancements, such as artificial intelligence and genetic engineering. It guides us in our interactions with people from diverse cultural backgrounds, promoting understanding and tolerance. It empowers us to speak out against injustice and inequality, striving for a more equitable and compassionate world.

Developing and strengthening our moral compass is an ongoing journey. It requires introspection, self-reflection, and a willingness to learn from our experiences. Engaging in thoughtful discussions with others, reading philosophical texts, and seeking guidance from mentors or role models can all contribute to the development of a well-rounded moral compass. Additionally, actively participating in community service and volunteering can foster empathy and compassion, further strengthening our moral core.

While a moral compass is an indispensable tool for navigating life's complexities, it's important to acknowledge that ethical dilemmas are not always black and white. Sometimes, there are competing values and principles at stake, and making the "right" decision can be challenging. In such situations, a moral compass provides a framework for evaluating the options, weighing the potential consequences, and making a choice that aligns with our deepest values.

A moral compass is not merely a philosophical concept; it's a practical and indispensable tool for leading a fulfilling and meaningful life. It guides our decisions, strengthens our relationships, fosters ethical behavior in society, and empowers us to make a positive impact on the world. As we navigate the ever-evolving landscape of the 21st century, a strong moral compass remains our most reliable guide, steering us toward a future where integrity, compassion, and justice prevail.

ppp

"A moral compass is not a mere accessory; it is the rudder that steers our ship through life's tumultuous seas. It is the inner voice that whispers guidance when faced with difficult choices, leading us toward a life of purpose and integrity."

TWO

BUILDING BLOCKS: CORE VALUES AND ETHICS

The foundation of a robust moral compass lies in the bedrock of core values and ethics. These fundamental principles act as the guiding lights, illuminating our path and shaping our decisions as we navigate the complexities of life. Much like the sturdy beams that support a well-constructed building, core values and ethics provide the structural integrity that enables us to stand tall in the face of challenges and make choices that align with our moral compass.

Core values are the deeply held beliefs that we consider most important in our lives. They represent our highest priorities and guide our actions, both big and small. These values can range from honesty, integrity, and respect to compassion, empathy, and fairness. While the specific values we hold dear may vary, they all serve a common purpose: to define who we are and what we stand for.

Ethics, on the other hand, are the moral principles that govern our behavior. They provide a framework for determining right and wrong, good and bad, just and unjust. Ethics are often derived from our core values and provide a practical application of those values in our daily lives. For example, if honesty is one of our core values, our ethics would dictate that we always tell the truth, even when it's difficult or inconvenient.

The interplay between core values and ethics is dynamic and mutually reinforcing. Our core values inform our ethical principles, and our ethical principles, in turn, reinforce our core values. This creates a virtuous cycle where our beliefs and actions continually strengthen and refine each other.

One of the most fundamental core values is honesty. Honesty is the cornerstone of trust, and trust is essential for building strong relationships and creating a just and equitable society. When we are honest with ourselves and others, we create an environment of transparency and authenticity where everyone can thrive.

Integrity is another essential core value. It means doing the right thing, even when no one is watching. It means upholding our values and principles, even when it's difficult or unpopular. Integrity is the foundation of character, and it's what allows us to earn the respect and admiration of others.

Respect is a core value that encompasses both self-respect and respect for others. When we respect ourselves, we value our own worth and dignity. When we respect others, we acknowledge their inherent worth and treat them with kindness and consideration. Respect is the basis for healthy relationships and a harmonious society.

Compassion is a core value that calls us to care for others and to act with empathy and kindness. It means recognizing the suffering of others and taking action to alleviate it. Compassion is the heart of humanity, and it's what allows us to connect with each other on a deeper level.

Fairness is a core value that requires us to treat everyone equally and justly. It means giving everyone a fair chance to succeed and not discriminating based on race, gender, religion, or any other factor. Fairness is the foundation of a just society, and it's what ensures that everyone has the opportunity to reach their full potential.

These are just a few examples of the many core values that can guide our lives. The specific values that we choose to embrace will depend on our individual beliefs and experiences. However, regardless of the specific values we hold dear, it's important to recognize that our core values are not static. They can evolve and change as we grow and learn.

The process of identifying and clarifying our core values is an ongoing journey of self-discovery. It requires introspection, reflection, and a willingness to confront our own biases and assumptions. It can be helpful to ask ourselves questions such as: What is most important to me? What do I stand for? What kind of person do I want to be? By taking the time to explore these questions, we can gain a deeper understanding of ourselves and our values.

Once we have identified our core values, it's important to integrate them into our daily lives. This means making decisions that align with our values and taking actions that reflect our beliefs. It also means being willing to stand up for our values, even when it's difficult or unpopular.

Living in accordance with our core values is not always easy, but it's the most rewarding path we can take. When we live a life of integrity, compassion, and fairness, we not only improve our own lives but also make the world a better place.

The building blocks of core values and ethics provide the foundation for a strong moral compass. When we take the time to identify and clarify our values, and when we live in accordance with those values, we create a life that is both meaningful and fulfilling. We also contribute to a more just and equitable society where everyone can thrive.

PPP

*"Empathy is the bridge that connects us to the
hearts and minds of others, allowing us to
understand their joys and sorrows, hopes and fears.
It is the foundation of compassion and the key to
building meaningful relationships."*

THREE

EMPATHY: UNDERSTANDING AND CONNECTING WITH OTHERS

Empathy, often described as the ability to understand and share the feelings of others, is a cornerstone of human interaction and a vital component of a well-developed moral compass. It is the bridge that connects us to the experiences and emotions of those around us, fostering compassion, understanding, and deeper connections. In a world that can sometimes feel isolating and divided, empathy serves as a powerful force for unity and positive change.

At its core, empathy involves stepping into the shoes of another person, seeing the world through their eyes, and feeling what they feel. It's not merely about sympathizing with someone's plight; it's about experiencing their emotions as if they were our own. This ability to connect with others on an emotional level is crucial for building meaningful relationships, resolving conflicts, and creating a more compassionate society.

The roots of empathy lie in our evolutionary history. As social creatures, our survival and well-being have always depended on our ability to cooperate and work together. Empathy allowed us to anticipate the needs of others, form alliances, and build cohesive communities. This innate capacity for empathy is evident even in young children, who often display spontaneous acts of kindness and concern for others.

Empathy manifests in different forms. Cognitive empathy involves understanding another person's perspective and recognizing their emotions. Affective empathy involves experiencing those emotions as if they were our own. And compassionate empathy goes beyond understanding and feeling; it motivates us to take action and help others in need.

The benefits of empathy are manifold. In our personal lives, empathy strengthens our relationships with friends, family, and romantic partners. It allows us to communicate more effectively, resolve conflicts peacefully, and provide support and comfort to those we care about. When we demonstrate empathy, we create a safe and supportive space for others to express their feelings and vulnerabilities, fostering deeper trust and intimacy.

In the workplace, empathy is an invaluable skill for leaders and team members alike. Empathetic leaders are better able to understand the needs and concerns of their employees, leading to increased job satisfaction, productivity, and collaboration. Empathetic team members are more likely to work together effectively, resolving disagreements and finding creative solutions to challenges.

Empathy also plays a crucial role in society as a whole. When we empathize with others, we are less likely to judge them harshly or stereotype them based on their background or circumstances. We are more likely to advocate for their rights and work towards creating a more equitable and inclusive society. Empathy is a powerful antidote to prejudice and discrimination, as it allows us to see the humanity in others, even those who are different from us.

The development of empathy is a lifelong journey. It requires self-awareness, active listening, and a willingness to challenge our own biases and assumptions. We can cultivate empathy by practicing mindfulness, engaging in meaningful conversations with others, reading literature that explores diverse perspectives, and volunteering in our communities.

It's important to note that empathy is not always easy. Sometimes, it can be painful to experience the suffering of others. We may feel overwhelmed or helpless in the face of their pain. However, it's important to remember that empathy is not about fixing other people's problems. It's about offering them understanding, support, and compassion.

In a world that can often feel chaotic and overwhelming, empathy provides a compass for navigating our relationships and making ethical decisions. It allows us to connect with others on a deeper level, build stronger communities, and create a more compassionate world. By cultivating empathy, we not only enrich our own lives but also contribute to the well-being of those around us.

As we face the challenges of the 21st century, the importance of empathy cannot be overstated. From addressing global issues like climate change and poverty to fostering understanding and cooperation between different cultures, empathy is an essential tool for building a better future for all. By embracing empathy as a guiding principle, we can create a world where compassion, understanding, and connection are the norm, rather than the exception.

ppp

"Honesty and integrity are the twin pillars of
character, the bedrock upon which trust is built.
They are the unwavering commitment to
truthfulness and ethical conduct, even when faced
with adversity."

FOUR

HONESTY AND INTEGRITY: SPEAKING TRUTH AND KEEPING PROMISES

Honesty and integrity, the twin pillars of moral character, are indispensable virtues that guide us towards a life of authenticity and trustworthiness. They are not merely words but fundamental principles that shape our actions, interactions, and relationships. When we embrace honesty and integrity, we cultivate a reputation for reliability, earn the respect of others, and contribute to a more just and ethical society.

Honesty, at its essence, is the act of speaking truth and living in alignment with reality. It involves being truthful in our words, actions, and intentions. Honesty is not merely the absence of lies; it is the active pursuit of truthfulness, even when it is difficult or uncomfortable. It requires us to be transparent and forthright in our communication, avoiding deception and misrepresentation.

The importance of honesty cannot be overstated. It is the foundation of trust, the glue that holds relationships together. When we are honest with others, we demonstrate respect for their autonomy and their right to know the truth. Honesty fosters open communication and allows for the free exchange of ideas and information. It creates an environment where individuals feel safe to express themselves authentically, leading to stronger connections and deeper understanding.

In the absence of honesty, trust erodes, and relationships crumble. Deception and dishonesty breed suspicion and resentment, creating a toxic atmosphere where genuine connection is impossible. Lies, no matter how small or seemingly insignificant, have a way of unraveling, causing harm not only to those we deceive but also to ourselves.

Integrity, closely intertwined with honesty, is the unwavering adherence to moral and ethical principles. It is the quality of being whole and undivided, living in accordance with our values and beliefs. Integrity is not simply about doing the right thing when it is convenient or advantageous; it is about consistently upholding our principles, even when faced with challenges or temptations.

Integrity is often tested in the face of adversity. It is easy to be honest and ethical when things are going well, but true integrity shines through during difficult times. When we are faced with a choice between compromising our values for personal gain or upholding our principles at a cost, integrity guides us towards the latter. It requires courage, resilience, and a steadfast commitment to our moral compass.

The benefits of integrity are far-reaching. It cultivates self-respect, as we know that we are living in alignment with our deepest values.

It earns us the respect and admiration of others, as they recognize our unwavering commitment to our principles. Integrity also fosters trust and credibility, making us reliable and dependable in the eyes of those around us.

In the professional realm, honesty and integrity are essential for building a successful and sustainable career. Ethical behavior is the cornerstone of any reputable organization, and employees who demonstrate honesty and integrity are valued assets. They are trusted with sensitive information, given greater responsibility, and seen as leaders within the company. Moreover, businesses with a strong ethical foundation are more likely to attract and retain customers, build a positive reputation, and thrive in the long run.

The ripple effects of honesty and integrity extend beyond our personal and professional lives. They contribute to the creation of a just and ethical society. When individuals uphold these values, communities flourish. Trust is established, cooperation is fostered, and conflicts are resolved peacefully. Honesty and integrity in public service ensure that government officials act in the best interests of the people they serve, promoting transparency and accountability.

In a world that can sometimes feel morally ambiguous, honesty and integrity provide a clear and unwavering guide. They remind us of the importance of truthfulness, ethical behavior, and personal responsibility. They challenge us to be our best selves, to live in accordance with our values, and to make choices that contribute to the greater good.

While the path of honesty and integrity may not always be easy, it is ultimately the most fulfilling and rewarding one. By embracing these virtues, we cultivate inner peace, build meaningful relationships, and contribute to a more just and ethical world. In the words of the renowned author C.S. Lewis, "Integrity is doing the right thing, even when no one is watching." Let us strive to embody this principle in all aspects of our lives, for it is through honesty and integrity that we truly find our moral compass.

🕊🕊🕊

"Respect is the cornerstone of human interaction, the recognition that every individual possesses inherent worth and deserves to be treated with dignity and consideration. It is the key to building harmonious relationships and fostering a just society."

FIVE

RESPECT: VALUING OURSELVES AND OTHERS

Respect, a cornerstone of human interaction and a fundamental moral value, encompasses a profound appreciation for the worth and dignity of both ourselves and others. It is the recognition that every individual, regardless of their background, beliefs, or circumstances, possesses inherent value and deserves to be treated with consideration, fairness, and kindness. Respect is not merely a social nicety; it is a moral imperative that underpins healthy relationships, fosters social harmony, and promotes personal growth.

At its core, respect involves valuing oneself and others as unique and autonomous beings. It means recognizing that each person has their own thoughts, feelings, experiences, and perspectives, and that these deserve to be acknowledged and honored. Respecting oneself entails setting healthy boundaries, advocating for one's needs, and refusing to tolerate mistreatment or disrespect from others. It means recognizing our own inherent worth and refusing to compromise our values or integrity.

Respecting others involves treating them with courtesy, kindness, and consideration. It means listening to their opinions, even if we disagree with them, and valuing their contributions. It means refraining from judgment, criticism, and ridicule, and instead focusing on understanding and appreciating their unique qualities. Respect for others also entails honoring their autonomy and allowing them to make their own choices, even if those choices differ from our own.

The practice of respect has a profound impact on our lives and the world around us. In our personal relationships, respect fosters trust, intimacy, and mutual understanding. When we feel respected by our partners, friends, and family members, we are more likely to open up, share our vulnerabilities, and deepen our connections. Respect creates a safe and supportive environment where individuals can express themselves authentically and feel valued for who they are.

In the workplace, respect is essential for creating a positive and productive atmosphere. When employees feel respected by their colleagues and supervisors, they are more engaged, motivated, and committed to their work. Respectful communication and collaboration lead to better decision-making, increased creativity, and improved problem-solving. A respectful workplace culture also reduces conflict, stress, and turnover, ultimately benefiting both employees and the organization as a whole.

Respect is also a critical component of social justice and equality. When we respect the inherent worth of all individuals, we are more likely to advocate for their rights and oppose discrimination and injustice. Respect for diversity and inclusivity allows us to learn from different perspectives, challenge our own biases, and build stronger, more resilient communities.

The cultivation of respect begins with self-reflection and a commitment to personal growth. It requires us to examine our own biases, prejudices, and assumptions, and to challenge any negative self-talk or self-limiting beliefs. We can foster self-respect by setting healthy boundaries, practicing self-care, and celebrating our achievements. We can also learn from role models who embody respect and strive to emulate their behavior.

Respecting others requires empathy, active listening, and a willingness to see the world through their eyes. It means putting aside our own ego and preconceived notions, and approaching others with an open mind and heart. We can practice respect by listening attentively to others, validating their feelings, and offering support and encouragement. We can also show respect by being mindful of our words and actions, avoiding gossip and negativity, and always treating others with kindness and consideration.

Teaching respect to children is essential for creating a more compassionate and equitable future. By modeling respectful behavior, encouraging open communication, and teaching children to value diversity and inclusivity, we can lay the foundation for a generation that embraces respect as a core value. Schools, families, and communities all have a role to play in fostering a culture of respect, where every individual feels valued and empowered.

In a world that can sometimes feel divided and polarized, respect serves as a unifying force. It reminds us of our shared humanity, our common struggles, and our collective aspirations. By embracing respect as a guiding principle, we can build bridges of understanding, heal wounds of division, and create a more just and compassionate society for all.

"Responsibility is not a burden but a privilege, the opportunity to shape our own lives and impact the world around us. It is the willingness to make thoughtful choices and accept the consequences of our actions."

SIX

RESPONSIBILITY: MAKING GOOD CHOICES AND OWNING OUR ACTIONS

Responsibility, a cornerstone of personal growth and ethical conduct, encompasses the ability to make thoughtful choices and accept the consequences of our actions. It is the understanding that we are not merely passive recipients of fate, but active agents who shape our own lives and impact the world around us. Embracing responsibility empowers us to navigate challenges, learn from our mistakes, and contribute positively to society.

At its core, responsibility involves making choices that align with our values and principles. It requires us to consider the potential consequences of our actions, both for ourselves and for others. Responsible decision-making involves weighing the available options, gathering information, and seeking guidance when needed. It means choosing the path that is most likely to lead to positive outcomes, even when it is difficult or unpopular.

In addition to making good choices, responsibility also entails owning our actions. This means accepting the consequences of our decisions, whether they are positive or negative. When we make mistakes, responsibility requires us to acknowledge our errors, apologize for any harm we have caused, and take steps to make amends. It means learning from our failures and using those lessons to guide our future choices.

The benefits of responsibility are numerous. It fosters personal growth and development, as we learn to take ownership of our lives and make choices that align with our goals and values. It also builds trust and respect in our relationships, as others come to rely on our dependability and accountability. Responsible individuals are valued in the workplace, as they are seen as reliable, trustworthy, and capable of handling challenging situations.

In the broader context of society, responsibility plays a crucial role in maintaining order and promoting well-being. When individuals take responsibility for their actions, communities thrive. Crime rates decrease, social cohesion increases, and people are more likely to help each other in times of need. Responsible citizens contribute to the greater good by volunteering their time and resources, supporting charitable causes, and advocating for social justice.

Responsibility is not always easy. It requires discipline, self-awareness, and a willingness to confront our own shortcomings. It can be tempting to blame others for our problems or to make excuses for our mistakes. However, true responsibility involves taking ownership of our lives and acknowledging the role we play in shaping our own destiny.

The cultivation of responsibility begins in childhood. As children grow and develop, they learn to make choices and experience the consequences of their actions. Parents and caregivers play a crucial role in teaching children about responsibility by setting clear expectations, providing guidance and support, and holding them accountable for their behavior. Schools also play a role in fostering responsibility by teaching children about citizenship, community service, and the importance of making ethical decisions.

As we mature, responsibility becomes increasingly important. In adulthood, we are faced with complex decisions that can have far-reaching consequences. Whether it's choosing a career path, starting a family, or engaging in civic life, responsible decision-making is essential for leading a fulfilling and meaningful life.

In today's interconnected world, responsibility takes on an even greater significance. Our actions can have a ripple effect, impacting not only those closest to us but also people and communities across the globe. The choices we make about consumption, environmental sustainability, and social justice have the power to shape the future of our planet and the well-being of generations to come.

Embracing responsibility is not merely a matter of personal ethics; it is a moral imperative. It is through responsible action that we can create a more just, equitable, and sustainable world. By making good choices, owning our actions, and taking responsibility for our lives, we contribute to a brighter future for ourselves, our communities, and the planet as a whole.

▷▷▷

"Fairness is the principle that guides us to treat everyone equally and justly, regardless of their background or circumstances. It is the recognition that every individual deserves a fair chance to succeed and to be treated with respect."

SEVEN

FAIRNESS: TREATING EVERYONE EQUALLY AND JUSTLY

Fairness, a cornerstone of ethical conduct and social harmony, embodies the principle of treating everyone equally and justly. It is the recognition that all individuals deserve to be treated with impartiality, regardless of their race, gender, socioeconomic status, or any other personal attribute. Fairness is not merely a matter of following rules or avoiding discrimination; it is a deep-seated value that guides our interactions with others, shapes our institutions, and contributes to the creation of a just and equitable society.

At its core, fairness involves recognizing the inherent worth and dignity of every individual. It means treating others with respect, compassion, and empathy, regardless of their background or circumstances. Fairness requires us to acknowledge that everyone has the right to be heard, to be treated with dignity, and to have their needs and interests considered.

The principle of fairness is often expressed as the Golden Rule: treat others as you would like to be treated. This simple yet profound maxim encapsulates the essence of fairness, encouraging us to put ourselves in the shoes of others and to consider how our actions might affect them. When we strive to treat others with the same level of respect, kindness, and consideration that we would want for ourselves, we create a more harmonious and equitable world.

Fairness is not always synonymous with equality. While equality implies treating everyone the same, fairness recognizes that individuals may have different needs and circumstances. In some cases, treating everyone equally may actually be unfair, as it fails to take into account the unique challenges and disadvantages that some individuals face. True fairness involves taking these differences into account and providing everyone with the resources and opportunities they need to succeed.

The concept of fairness is deeply intertwined with the notion of justice. Justice is the principle of upholding what is right and fair, especially in the distribution of rewards and punishments. Fairness is an essential component of justice, as it ensures that everyone is treated impartially and that decisions are made based on merit, not on personal biases or prejudices.

Fairness is a critical component of a healthy and functioning society. When individuals feel that they are being treated fairly, they are more likely to trust their institutions, obey the law, and participate in civic life. Fairness fosters social cohesion, reduces conflict, and promotes cooperation. It creates an environment where individuals feel valued and empowered, leading to increased innovation, productivity, and overall well-being.

In the absence of fairness, societies become fractured and unstable. Inequality, discrimination, and injustice breed resentment, anger, and distrust. Social unrest and conflict can arise when individuals feel that their voices are not being heard or that their rights are being violated. A lack of fairness can also lead to economic instability, as marginalized groups are denied access to education, employment, and other opportunities.

The pursuit of fairness is an ongoing challenge. It requires us to constantly examine our own biases and prejudices, to challenge systemic inequalities, and to advocate for policies and practices that promote equal opportunity for all. It involves working together to build a more just and equitable society, where everyone has the chance to reach their full potential.

Fairness is not just a matter of abstract principles; it has real-world consequences. In the workplace, fair treatment leads to increased employee morale, productivity, and loyalty. In the legal system, fairness ensures that everyone receives a fair trial and that justice is served. In education, fairness means providing all students with the resources and support they need to succeed, regardless of their background or circumstances.

Fairness is also essential in our personal relationships. When we treat our friends, family members, and romantic partners with fairness, we build trust, strengthen our bonds, and create a more harmonious and fulfilling life. Fairness in our interactions with others demonstrates respect for their autonomy, their feelings, and their needs.

In a world that can often feel unfair and unjust, it is easy to become cynical and lose hope. However, the pursuit of fairness is not a futile endeavor. By recognizing the inherent worth of every individual, challenging systemic inequalities, and advocating for policies and practices that promote equal opportunity, we can create a more just and equitable world. Fairness is not just a moral imperative; it is a practical necessity for building a society where everyone can thrive.

ᡃᡃᡃ

"Compassion is the heart of humanity, the ability to feel deeply for the suffering of others and to be moved to action. It is the driving force behind acts of kindness, generosity, and love."

EIGHT

Compassion: Showing Kindness and Caring for Others

Compassion, the profound feeling of deep sympathy and sorrow for another who is stricken by misfortune, accompanied by a strong desire to alleviate the suffering, is an essential ingredient for a meaningful and ethical life. It is the emotional capacity that allows us to connect with the pain and suffering of others, to see their humanity, and to respond with kindness, care, and support. In a world that can often feel harsh and indifferent, compassion serves as a beacon of hope, reminding us of our shared vulnerability and our interconnectedness.

At its core, compassion involves recognizing the suffering of others and feeling moved to alleviate it. It is not merely about feeling sorry for someone; it is about experiencing a deep sense of empathy and concern for their well-being. Compassion goes beyond sympathy, which is the ability to understand another person's feelings, and empathy, which is the ability to share those feelings. Compassion is the emotional response that motivates us to take action and help others in need.

The roots of compassion can be traced back to our evolutionary history. As social creatures, our survival and well-being have always depended on our ability to cooperate and care for each other. Compassion allowed us to form strong bonds with others, to protect the vulnerable, and to ensure the survival of our communities. This innate capacity for compassion is evident even in young children, who often display spontaneous acts of kindness and concern for others.

Compassion manifests in different ways. It can be expressed through words of comfort and encouragement, acts of service and support, or simply by being present and listening to someone in need. Compassion can be directed towards individuals, groups, or even entire communities. It is not limited to those we know or those who are similar to us; it extends to all beings who are capable of suffering.

The benefits of compassion are manifold. In our personal lives, compassion strengthens our relationships with others. When we show compassion towards our friends, family, and romantic partners, we create a sense of trust, safety, and belonging. We also experience greater happiness and well-being, as research has shown that compassionate individuals tend to have lower levels of stress and anxiety, stronger immune systems, and greater life satisfaction.

In the workplace, compassion fosters a positive and productive work environment. When leaders and colleagues demonstrate compassion towards each other, it creates a culture of trust, support, and collaboration. Employees who feel valued and cared for are more engaged, motivated, and productive. Compassionate workplaces also experience lower rates of absenteeism, turnover, and burnout.

Compassion also plays a crucial role in society as a whole. When we extend compassion to those who are marginalized, oppressed, or suffering, we create a more just and equitable world. Compassion motivates us to advocate for social change, to fight for the rights of others, and to work towards creating a society where everyone has the opportunity to thrive.

The cultivation of compassion is a lifelong journey. It requires self-awareness, mindfulness, and a willingness to confront our own biases and prejudices. We can cultivate compassion by practicing meditation and mindfulness, engaging in acts of kindness and service, and reading literature that explores the experiences of others. We can also learn from role models who embody compassion and strive to emulate their behavior.

It is important to note that compassion is not always easy. It can be painful to witness the suffering of others, and we may feel overwhelmed or helpless in the face of their pain. However, it is precisely in these moments that compassion is most needed. By offering a listening ear, a helping hand, or simply a kind word, we can make a profound difference in the lives of others.

In a world that can often feel divided and polarized, compassion serves as a unifying force. It reminds us of our shared humanity, our common struggles, and our collective capacity for love and kindness. By embracing compassion as a guiding principle, we can build bridges of understanding, heal wounds of division, and create a more just, equitable, and compassionate world for all.

ppp

"Courage is not the absence of fear, but the triumph over it. It is the unwavering resolve to stand up for what is right, even in the face of danger or opposition."

NINE

COURAGE: STANDING UP FOR WHAT IS RIGHT

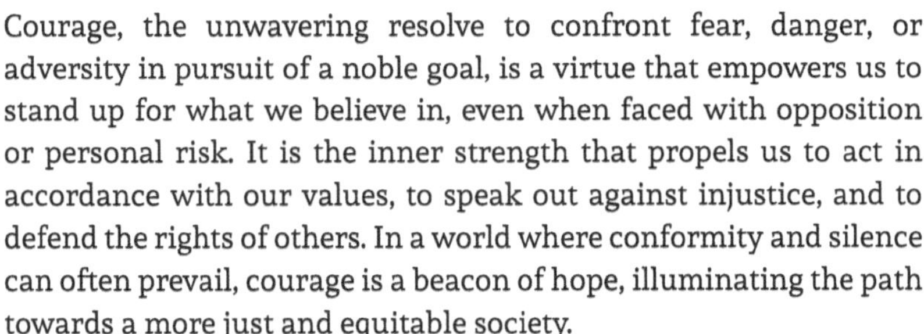

Courage, the unwavering resolve to confront fear, danger, or adversity in pursuit of a noble goal, is a virtue that empowers us to stand up for what we believe in, even when faced with opposition or personal risk. It is the inner strength that propels us to act in accordance with our values, to speak out against injustice, and to defend the rights of others. In a world where conformity and silence can often prevail, courage is a beacon of hope, illuminating the path towards a more just and equitable society.

At its core, courage is not the absence of fear but the triumph over it. It is the ability to acknowledge our fears, to confront them head-on, and to act despite them. Courageous individuals are not immune to fear; they simply refuse to let fear dictate their actions. They possess a deep-seated belief in the importance of their cause, a conviction that compels them to persevere in the face of adversity.

The manifestations of courage are diverse. It can be found in the soldier who charges into battle to defend their country, the activist who speaks out against oppression, the whistleblower who exposes corruption, or the ordinary citizen who stands up to a bully. Courage can also be found in smaller, everyday acts of bravery, such as speaking up for a friend who is being mistreated, admitting a mistake, or pursuing a dream despite the odds.

Courage is not a one-size-fits-all concept. What may require courage for one person may not for another. The challenges we face are unique to our individual circumstances, and the courage we need to overcome them will vary accordingly. However, regardless of the specific situation, courage always involves facing our fears and acting in accordance with our values.

The benefits of courage are immeasurable. It empowers us to live authentically, to be true to ourselves and our beliefs. It allows us to make a difference in the world, to stand up for what is right, and to fight for a better future. Courageous individuals inspire others, ignite hope, and catalyze change. They show us that it is possible to overcome adversity, to challenge the status quo, and to create a more just and equitable society.

The cultivation of courage is an ongoing process. It requires self-reflection, introspection, and a willingness to confront our fears and insecurities. We can cultivate courage by identifying our values, setting goals that align with those values, and taking small steps towards achieving those goals. We can also learn from role models who embody courage, studying their lives and emulating their behavior.

It is important to note that courage is not reckless or impulsive. It is not about taking unnecessary risks or acting without regard for consequences. True courage involves careful consideration, strategic planning, and a willingness to accept the potential costs of our actions. It is a calculated risk, taken in pursuit of a greater good.

Courage is not always rewarded with immediate success. Sometimes, courageous individuals face setbacks, persecution, and even death. However, their actions often plant the seeds for future change, inspiring others to take up the mantle and continue the fight for justice. The legacy of courageous individuals lives on long after they are gone, reminding us of the power of one person to make a difference.

In a world that can sometimes feel overwhelming and disheartening, courage provides a beacon of hope. It reminds us that we are not powerless, that we have the ability to shape our own destinies and to contribute to a better future. By embracing courage, we can overcome our fears, stand up for what we believe in, and create a world that is more just, equitable, and compassionate.

ϷϷϷ

"Perseverance is the key to unlocking our full potential, the ability to overcome obstacles and setbacks with unwavering determination. It is the fuel that propels us towards our goals and dreams."

TEN

PERSEVERANCE: NEVER GIVING UP ON DOING GOOD

Perseverance, the unwavering determination to pursue a course of action, a belief, or a goal despite obstacles, difficulties, or discouragement, is a virtue that underpins human achievement and moral fortitude. It is the relentless pursuit of good, the refusal to succumb to setbacks, and the unwavering belief in the possibility of positive change. In a world where challenges abound and progress can often seem elusive, perseverance serves as a guiding light, reminding us that even the most daunting obstacles can be overcome with unwavering commitment and resilience.

At its core, perseverance is the embodiment of grit, the tenacity to keep going when the going gets tough. It is the refusal to accept defeat, the ability to bounce back from failure, and the unwavering belief that our efforts will eventually bear fruit. Perseverance is not simply about stubbornness or blind determination; it is about maintaining hope and optimism in the face of adversity, drawing strength from our values and beliefs, and finding creative solutions to overcome challenges.

The importance of perseverance is evident in all walks of life. In the realm of personal development, perseverance is the key to achieving our goals and realizing our full potential. Whether it is learning a new skill, overcoming a personal challenge, or pursuing a lifelong dream, perseverance allows us to push past our limits and achieve what we once thought impossible. It is the driving force behind every great accomplishment, from the scientist who toils for years to discover a breakthrough cure to the athlete who trains relentlessly to win a championship.

In the realm of social justice and activism, perseverance is an indispensable virtue. Those who fight for equality, human rights, and a more just society often face formidable obstacles, from entrenched power structures to public apathy. Perseverance allows them to continue their struggle despite setbacks and disappointments, to maintain their hope for a better future, and to inspire others to join their cause. The history of social progress is replete with examples of individuals and movements that achieved significant change through unwavering perseverance.

Perseverance is also a vital ingredient in the pursuit of knowledge and understanding. The path of learning is often fraught with challenges, from complex theories to demanding coursework. Perseverance allows students to overcome these obstacles, to master new concepts, and to develop the skills and knowledge they need to succeed in their chosen fields. It is the quality that separates those who merely dabble in a subject from those who achieve mastery.

In the realm of personal relationships, perseverance is essential for building strong and lasting bonds. Relationships inevitably encounter challenges, from disagreements and misunderstandings to external pressures and life transitions. Perseverance allows us to work through these difficulties, to communicate openly and honestly, and to find solutions that strengthen our connections. It is the glue that holds relationships together during tough times, allowing them to grow and deepen over time.

The cultivation of perseverance is an ongoing process. It requires developing mental resilience, cultivating a positive mindset, and learning from our failures. We can foster perseverance by setting realistic goals, breaking down large tasks into smaller, more manageable steps, and celebrating our successes along the way. We can also draw inspiration from role models who have demonstrated remarkable perseverance in their own lives, learning from their experiences and applying their strategies to our own challenges.

It is important to recognize that perseverance is not about brute force or relentless effort. It is about working smarter, not harder. It involves finding creative solutions, adapting to changing circumstances, and knowing when to ask for help. Perseverance also requires self-care, as we need to replenish our energy and maintain our well-being in order to continue our journey.

In a world that can often seem chaotic and unpredictable, perseverance provides a sense of stability and purpose. It allows us to focus on our goals, to overcome obstacles, and to create a meaningful life. By embracing perseverance, we not only enhance our own lives but also contribute to the well-being of our communities and the world as a whole. Perseverance is a gift that we give to ourselves and to future generations, a testament to the power of the human spirit to overcome adversity and achieve greatness.

ppp

"Gratitude is the art of appreciating the blessings in our lives, both big and small. It is the recognition that we are surrounded by abundance, even in the midst of challenges."

ELEVEN

GRATITUDE: APPRECIATING WHAT WE HAVE

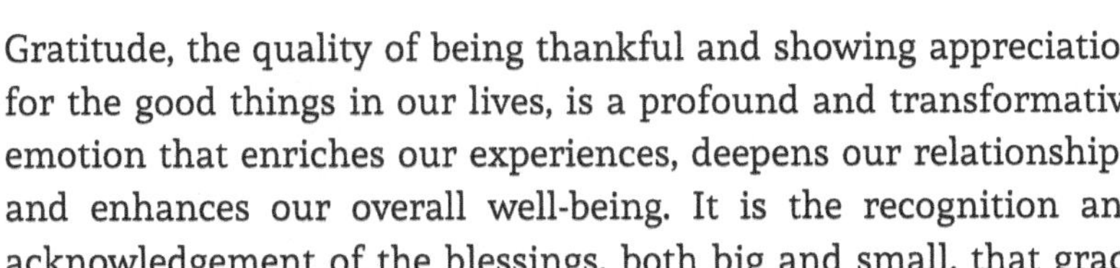

Gratitude, the quality of being thankful and showing appreciation for the good things in our lives, is a profound and transformative emotion that enriches our experiences, deepens our relationships, and enhances our overall well-being. It is the recognition and acknowledgement of the blessings, both big and small, that grace our existence. In a world that often focuses on what we lack, gratitude serves as a powerful antidote, shifting our perspective towards abundance and contentment.

At its core, gratitude is a state of mind, a way of perceiving the world through a lens of appreciation. It involves recognizing the value and significance of the positive aspects of our lives, whether they be material possessions, relationships, experiences, or personal qualities. Gratitude is not simply about being thankful for the extraordinary or exceptional; it is about finding joy and meaning in the ordinary, everyday moments that make up our lives.

The practice of gratitude has a profound impact on our emotional, mental, and physical well-being. Research has shown that grateful individuals tend to be happier, more optimistic, and less prone to depression and anxiety. Gratitude also enhances our resilience, helping us to cope with stress and adversity more effectively. It strengthens our relationships, as expressing gratitude towards others fosters connection, trust, and intimacy. Gratitude even has positive effects on our physical health, boosting our immune system, improving sleep quality, and reducing blood pressure.

The benefits of gratitude extend beyond our personal lives. Gratitude can transform our workplaces, making them more positive, productive, and collaborative. When employees feel appreciated and valued, they are more engaged, motivated, and committed to their work. Gratitude can also improve customer satisfaction, as grateful employees are more likely to provide excellent service and go the extra mile to meet customer needs.

Gratitude can also have a positive impact on our communities. When we express gratitude towards others, we create a ripple effect of kindness and generosity. Gratitude inspires us to give back to our communities, to volunteer our time and resources, and to support causes that we care about. A culture of gratitude can transform neighborhoods, schools, and workplaces into more supportive and inclusive environments.

The cultivation of gratitude is a lifelong journey. It requires a conscious effort to shift our focus from what we lack to what we have. We can cultivate gratitude by practicing mindfulness, paying attention to the present moment, and noticing the small joys and blessings that surround us. We can keep a gratitude journal, where we write down three things we are grateful for each day. We can also express our gratitude to others, through words of affirmation, acts of kindness, or simply by spending quality time with them.

It is important to note that gratitude is not about denying or ignoring the challenges and difficulties we face in life. It is about recognizing that even in the midst of adversity, there are still things to be grateful for. Gratitude does not erase our problems, but it can help us to see them in a new light, to find strength and resilience in the face of adversity, and to appreciate the lessons that challenges can teach us.

In a world that often bombards us with negative messages and encourages us to focus on what we lack, gratitude offers a refreshing alternative. It reminds us that we are not defined by our possessions or our achievements, but by our capacity for love, kindness, and appreciation. By embracing gratitude, we can cultivate a more positive outlook on life, deepen our connections with others, and make a meaningful contribution to the world.

"Forgiveness is the gift we give to ourselves and others, the release of anger and resentment that allows us to heal and move forward. It is the path towards reconciliation, peace, and inner freedom."

TWELVE

FORGIVENESS: HEALING HURTS AND LETTING GO

Forgiveness, the act of pardoning an offense, fault, or mistake, is a profound and transformative process that liberates both the giver and the receiver from the shackles of resentment, anger, and pain. It is not merely about forgetting or condoning hurtful actions; it is about acknowledging the wrong, accepting the apology, and choosing to release the negative emotions associated with the transgression. Forgiveness is a gift we give to ourselves and others, paving the path towards healing, reconciliation, and inner peace.

At its core, forgiveness is a conscious and deliberate decision to let go of the anger, resentment, and desire for revenge that often accompany being hurt or wronged. It is not an act of weakness or naivety; it requires courage, strength, and a willingness to confront painful emotions. Forgiveness does not mean forgetting the past or condoning the offense; rather, it allows us to acknowledge the harm done, to process our emotions, and to move forward without being consumed by bitterness and resentment.

ppp

The benefits of forgiveness are manifold. It liberates us from the burden of anger and resentment, allowing us to experience emotional healing and inner peace. When we forgive, we break free from the cycle of pain and negativity, opening ourselves up to the possibility of joy, compassion, and connection. Forgiveness also has positive effects on our physical health, reducing stress, lowering blood pressure, and boosting our immune system.

Forgiveness is not only beneficial for the forgiver, but also for the forgiven. When we extend forgiveness to someone who has wronged us, we offer them a chance to redeem themselves and to rebuild trust. Forgiveness can repair broken relationships, mend wounds, and pave the way for reconciliation. It is a powerful act of grace that can transform lives and create a ripple effect of positive change.

The process of forgiveness is not always easy. It can be a long and arduous journey, requiring patience, self-reflection, and a willingness to confront painful emotions. However, the rewards are immeasurable. Forgiveness liberates us from the past, allowing us to live fully in the present and to embrace the future with hope and optimism.

Forgiveness can be extended to others, as well as to ourselves. Self-forgiveness is the act of accepting our own mistakes and shortcomings, of acknowledging our humanity and our capacity for growth. It involves letting go of guilt, shame, and self-blame, and embracing self-compassion and understanding. Self-forgiveness is essential for personal growth and development, as it allows us to learn from our mistakes and move forward with a renewed sense of purpose and direction.

Forgiveness is not a one-time event; it is an ongoing process. It may take time to fully forgive someone, and there may be setbacks along the way. However, with patience, perseverance, and a willingness to engage in the process, forgiveness is possible. There are many resources available to help individuals on their journey towards forgiveness, including therapy, support groups, and spiritual guidance.

In a world that is often characterized by conflict, division, and resentment, forgiveness offers a powerful alternative. It is a path towards healing, reconciliation, and a more compassionate and understanding world. By embracing forgiveness, we not only liberate ourselves from the pain of the past, but we also contribute to the creation of a more peaceful and harmonious future.

Forgiveness is not a sign of weakness; it is a testament to our strength and resilience. It takes courage to forgive, to let go of anger and resentment, and to choose love over hate. When we forgive, we demonstrate our capacity for compassion, empathy, and understanding. We become agents of healing, both for ourselves and for others.

ᗞᗞᗞ

"Cooperation is the key to unlocking our collective potential, the recognition that we are stronger together than we are alone. It is the willingness to collaborate, compromise, and work towards shared goals."

THIRTEEN

COOPERATION: WORKING TOGETHER FOR THE GREATER GOOD

Cooperation, the act of working together for a common purpose or benefit, is a fundamental human behavior that has enabled us to achieve remarkable feats throughout history. It is the driving force behind the creation of complex societies, the development of groundbreaking technologies, and the resolution of global challenges. Cooperation is not merely a matter of convenience or practicality; it is an essential ingredient for human flourishing and a key component of a well-functioning society.

At its core, cooperation involves recognizing that we are stronger together than we are alone. It is the understanding that by pooling our resources, knowledge, and skills, we can achieve far more than we ever could individually. Cooperation requires us to put aside our differences, to find common ground, and to work towards shared goals. It involves communication, compromise, and a willingness to share credit and responsibility.

The benefits of cooperation are manifold. In our personal lives, cooperation strengthens our relationships with friends, family, and community members. When we work together, we build trust, foster mutual respect, and create a sense of belonging. Cooperation also allows us to share resources, knowledge, and skills, leading to greater efficiency and productivity. In the workplace, cooperation is essential for achieving organizational goals. When teams work together effectively, they are able to leverage their diverse talents and perspectives, leading to better decision-making, increased creativity, and improved problem-solving. Cooperative workplaces also tend to have higher levels of employee satisfaction, engagement, and retention.

On a societal level, cooperation is crucial for addressing complex challenges such as climate change, poverty, and conflict. No single individual or organization can solve these problems alone. Cooperation between governments, businesses, non-profit organizations, and individuals is essential for developing and implementing effective solutions. When we work together, we can pool our resources, knowledge, and expertise to tackle these challenges head-on.

Cooperation also plays a vital role in promoting peace and stability. When countries cooperate, they are less likely to engage in conflict. Cooperation can lead to the establishment of international agreements, the sharing of resources, and the development of joint initiatives to address common concerns. By working together, nations can build trust, reduce tensions, and create a more peaceful and prosperous world.

The cultivation of cooperation is an ongoing process. It requires us to develop empathy, communication skills, and a willingness to compromise. We can foster cooperation by actively listening to others, valuing their perspectives, and seeking common ground. We can also practice collaboration and teamwork, working together to achieve shared goals.

It is important to recognize that cooperation is not always easy. It can be challenging to overcome our differences, to compromise our own interests for the sake of the group, and to trust others to do their part. However, the rewards of cooperation are far greater than the challenges. When we cooperate, we tap into our collective potential and achieve remarkable feats. We build stronger relationships, create more effective organizations, and contribute to a better world.

In a world that is often characterized by competition and individualism, cooperation offers a refreshing alternative. It reminds us that we are not isolated individuals, but interconnected beings who rely on each other for survival and well-being. By embracing cooperation, we can tap into our collective wisdom, creativity, and resilience. We can overcome challenges, achieve our goals, and create a more just, equitable, and sustainable world for all.

ppp

"*Self-discipline is the master key to success, the ability to control our thoughts, emotions, and actions in pursuit of our goals. It is the inner strength that allows us to resist temptation and stay focused on what truly matters.*"

FOURTEEN

SELF-DISCIPLINE: CONTROLLING OUR THOUGHTS AND ACTIONS

Self-discipline, the ability to control one's thoughts, emotions, and actions in pursuit of desired outcomes, is a cornerstone of personal growth, achievement, and moral fortitude. It is the inner strength that allows us to resist temptations, overcome obstacles, and persevere in the face of adversity. Self-discipline is not about denying ourselves pleasure or living a life of deprivation; it is about making conscious choices that align with our values and goals, even when those choices are difficult or uncomfortable.

At its core, self-discipline is the practice of self-regulation. It involves recognizing our impulses, desires, and emotions, and choosing to act in accordance with our long-term interests rather than succumbing to short-term gratification. Self-discipline is not something we are born with; it is a skill that we develop and strengthen over time through practice and perseverance.

The importance of self-discipline is evident in all areas of life. In our personal lives, self-discipline allows us to establish healthy habits, achieve our goals, and maintain our well-being. It empowers us to make choices that are in our best interests, even when those choices are difficult or unpopular. Whether it's waking up early to exercise, sticking to a budget, or pursuing a passion project, self-discipline is the key to achieving our full potential.

In the workplace, self-discipline is essential for success. It allows us to focus our attention, manage our time effectively, and produce high-quality work. Self-disciplined individuals are able to resist distractions, meet deadlines, and maintain their composure under pressure. They are seen as reliable, trustworthy, and capable of handling challenging tasks.

In the realm of relationships, self-discipline plays a crucial role in maintaining healthy connections. It allows us to control our emotions, to communicate effectively, and to resolve conflicts constructively. Self-disciplined individuals are less likely to engage in impulsive or destructive behavior that can damage relationships. They are also more likely to be supportive, understanding, and respectful of their partners, friends, and family members.

Self-discipline is also a key component of moral character. It allows us to act in accordance with our values and principles, even when tempted to do otherwise. Self-disciplined individuals are less likely to succumb to peer pressure, to engage in unethical behavior, or to compromise their integrity for personal gain. They are guided by a strong sense of right and wrong, and they strive to live in a way that is consistent with their moral compass.

The cultivation of self-discipline is a lifelong journey. It requires self-awareness, introspection, and a willingness to confront our weaknesses. It also requires patience, perseverance, and a belief in our own ability to change. There are many strategies that can help us develop and strengthen our self-discipline. Setting clear goals, creating a plan of action, and tracking our progress are all effective ways to stay motivated and on track.

It is also important to develop healthy coping mechanisms for dealing with stress and temptation. Meditation, mindfulness, and exercise can all help us to manage our emotions and resist impulsive behavior. Seeking support from friends, family, or a therapist can also be helpful.

The benefits of self-discipline are immeasurable. It empowers us to take control of our lives, to achieve our goals, and to live in accordance with our values. Self-disciplined individuals are happier, healthier, and more successful in all areas of life. They are also more resilient in the face of adversity, as they have the inner strength to overcome challenges and setbacks.

In a world that is constantly bombarding us with distractions and temptations, self-discipline is more important than ever. It is the key to achieving our full potential, to building meaningful relationships, and to making a positive impact on the world. By embracing self-discipline as a way of life, we can create a future that is brighter, healthier, and more fulfilling.

ϷϷϷ

"Humility is the recognition that we are not the center of the universe, that we are part of something much larger than ourselves. It is the willingness to learn from others, to acknowledge our limitations, and to celebrate the achievements of others."

FIFTEEN

Humility: Recognizing Our Strengths and Weaknesses

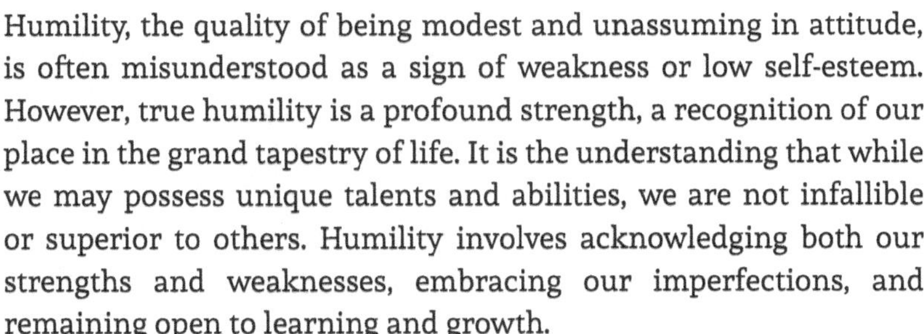

Humility, the quality of being modest and unassuming in attitude, is often misunderstood as a sign of weakness or low self-esteem. However, true humility is a profound strength, a recognition of our place in the grand tapestry of life. It is the understanding that while we may possess unique talents and abilities, we are not infallible or superior to others. Humility involves acknowledging both our strengths and weaknesses, embracing our imperfections, and remaining open to learning and growth.

At its core, humility is the antithesis of arrogance and pride. It is the recognition that our achievements are not solely the result of our own efforts, but are often influenced by factors beyond our control, such as luck, opportunity, and the support of others. Humility does not diminish our accomplishments; rather, it contextualizes them within a broader perspective, acknowledging the contributions of others and the role of circumstance.

Humility is not about denying our strengths or downplaying our accomplishments. It is about recognizing that we are not perfect, that we have limitations, and that we are always capable of learning and improving. Humility involves acknowledging our weaknesses, seeking feedback from others, and being open to constructive criticism. It is the understanding that we can always strive to be better, both as individuals and as members of society.

The benefits of humility are numerous. It fosters healthy relationships, as humble individuals are more approachable, empathetic, and understanding. They are less likely to judge or criticize others, and more likely to offer support and encouragement. Humility also enhances our ability to learn and grow, as we are more open to feedback and new ideas. Humble individuals are often seen as more trustworthy and credible, as their lack of arrogance and self-importance inspires confidence and respect.

In the workplace, humility is a valuable asset for leaders and team members alike. Humble leaders are more likely to listen to the ideas of others, to acknowledge their own mistakes, and to share credit for successes. This creates a more positive and collaborative work environment, where employees feel valued and empowered. Humble team members are more likely to be open to feedback, to learn from their mistakes, and to work collaboratively with others towards shared goals.

Humility also plays a crucial role in our personal lives. It allows us to form deeper and more meaningful connections with others, as we are more willing to be vulnerable and authentic. Humble individuals are less likely to be consumed by ego and self-importance, and more likely to focus on the needs of others. This can lead to greater happiness and fulfillment, as we find meaning and purpose in serving others and contributing to the greater good.

The cultivation of humility is an ongoing process. It requires self-reflection, introspection, and a willingness to confront our own ego and pride. We can cultivate humility by practicing gratitude, acknowledging the contributions of others, and focusing on our own growth and development. We can also learn from role models who embody humility, studying their lives and emulating their behavior.

It is important to note that humility is not synonymous with low self-esteem or self-deprecation. While humility involves recognizing our weaknesses, it also involves acknowledging our strengths and celebrating our accomplishments. Humility is not about putting ourselves down; it is about recognizing our place in the world and appreciating the interconnectedness of all things.

In a world that often values competition, individualism, and self-promotion, humility offers a refreshing alternative. It reminds us that we are not defined by our achievements or our possessions, but by our character, our values, and our relationships. By embracing humility, we can cultivate a more grounded, compassionate, and fulfilling life. We can also contribute to a more harmonious and equitable society, where everyone is valued and respected for their unique contributions.

ᴘᴘᴘ

"Generosity is the art of giving freely, without expecting anything in return. It is the expression of love, kindness, and compassion towards others. It is the recognition that we have more than enough to share."

SIXTEEN

GENEROSITY: SHARING OUR TIME, TALENTS, AND RESOURCES

Generosity, the act of giving and sharing freely, is a virtue that enriches both the giver and the receiver. It is the willingness to extend ourselves beyond our own needs and desires, to offer our time, talents, and resources for the benefit of others. Generosity is not merely about material giving; it is a spirit of selflessness, compassion, and a deep understanding of our interconnectedness. In a world that often emphasizes individualism and competition, generosity serves as a powerful antidote, fostering connection, empathy, and a sense of shared humanity.

At its core, generosity is the act of giving without expecting anything in return. It is a selfless expression of love, kindness, and compassion. Generosity can manifest in many forms, from offering a helping hand to a stranger to donating to a charitable cause. It can be expressed through our time, our talents, our resources, or simply our words of encouragement and support.

The act of giving is not only beneficial for the recipient but also for the giver. Research has shown that generosity can have a profound impact on our well-being, both mentally and physically. When we give to others, our brains release endorphins, dopamine, and serotonin, neurochemicals that promote happiness, reduce stress, and boost our immune system. Generosity has also been linked to lower levels of depression, anxiety, and chronic pain.

Generosity is not only good for our health; it is also essential for building strong and meaningful relationships. When we give to others, we demonstrate our care and concern for their well-being. This strengthens our bonds with them, fosters trust, and creates a sense of reciprocity. Generosity can also help to repair damaged relationships, as it shows a willingness to forgive and move forward.

In the workplace, generosity can create a more positive and collaborative environment. When employees are willing to share their knowledge, skills, and resources with each other, it fosters a culture of learning and growth. Generosity can also improve teamwork and collaboration, as it encourages individuals to work together towards common goals.

Generosity also has a positive impact on our communities. When we give to charitable causes, volunteer our time, or simply offer a helping hand to those in need, we contribute to the well-being of our communities and make them more vibrant and resilient. Generosity can also inspire others to give, creating a ripple effect of kindness and compassion.

The cultivation of generosity is an ongoing process. It requires us to be mindful of the needs of others, to be willing to let go of our own attachments, and to embrace a spirit of abundance. We can cultivate generosity by practicing gratitude, reflecting on the blessings in our own lives, and recognizing that we have more than enough to share.

It is important to note that generosity is not about giving until it hurts. It is about finding a balance between our own needs and the needs of others. We can all find ways to be generous, no matter how much time, talent, or resources we have to offer. Even small acts of kindness can make a big difference in the lives of others.

In a world that can often feel divided and competitive, generosity offers a powerful antidote. It reminds us that we are all connected, that we are all part of something bigger than ourselves. By embracing generosity, we can create a more compassionate, equitable, and fulfilling world for all.

ᗡᗡᗡ

"The Golden Rule is a timeless principle that transcends cultural boundaries, a universal call to treat others with the same kindness and respect that we desire for ourselves. It is the foundation of ethical conduct and the key to building harmonious relationships."

SEVENTEEN

THE GOLDEN RULE: TREATING OTHERS AS WE WANT TO BE TREATED

The Golden Rule, a timeless ethical principle found in various forms across cultures and religions, encapsulates the essence of reciprocity and empathy in human interactions. It is a simple yet profound maxim that guides us to treat others with the same kindness, consideration, and respect that we desire for ourselves. The Golden Rule is not merely a religious doctrine; it is a universal principle that transcends cultural boundaries and speaks to the fundamental values of compassion, fairness, and human dignity.

At its core, the Golden Rule is a call to empathy, urging us to put ourselves in the shoes of others and to imagine how our actions might affect them. It challenges us to consider the impact of our words and deeds on those around us, and to act in ways that promote understanding, harmony, and mutual respect. The Golden Rule is not a rigid set of rules; rather, it is a guiding principle that encourages us to reflect on our own desires and values, and to extend those same considerations to others.

The Golden Rule has been expressed in various ways throughout history. In the Christian tradition, it is often quoted as "Do unto others as you would have them do unto you." Similar expressions can be found in other religions, such as the Jewish principle of "Love your neighbor as yourself" and the Islamic teaching of "None of you truly believes until he loves for his brother what he loves for himself." While the wording may vary, the underlying message remains the same: treat others with the same kindness and respect that you would want for yourself.

The Golden Rule is not merely a theoretical concept; it has practical implications for our daily lives. It guides us in our interactions with family, friends, colleagues, and even strangers. It encourages us to be kind, compassionate, and understanding, even when faced with difficult or challenging situations. The Golden Rule reminds us that we are all interconnected, that our actions have consequences for others, and that by treating others well, we create a more positive and harmonious world.

The application of the Golden Rule can be seen in countless ways. It guides us to be honest and truthful in our dealings with others, to be respectful of their opinions and beliefs, and to refrain from causing harm or injustice. It encourages us to offer help and support to those in need, to forgive those who have wronged us, and to strive for reconciliation and understanding. The Golden Rule can also be applied in the workplace, where it promotes ethical business practices, fair treatment of employees, and a commitment to social responsibility.

The Golden Rule is not without its challenges. It can be difficult to consistently apply this principle in our lives, especially when we are faced with individuals who do not reciprocate our kindness or respect. However, the Golden Rule is not about expecting others to behave in a certain way; it is about choosing to act in a way that aligns with our own values and principles, regardless of the actions of others.

The Golden Rule is also not a license to impose our own values or beliefs on others. It is about recognizing the inherent worth and dignity of every individual, and treating them with respect, even if we disagree with their choices or lifestyle. The Golden Rule encourages us to seek common ground, to find ways to coexist peacefully, and to build bridges of understanding between different cultures and communities.

The Golden Rule is a powerful tool for personal growth and development. By striving to live in accordance with this principle, we cultivate empathy, compassion, and a deeper understanding of ourselves and others. We learn to see the world through the eyes of others, to appreciate their perspectives, and to find common ground even in the midst of disagreement.

The Golden Rule is not a new concept, but its message is as relevant today as it was centuries ago. In a world that is increasingly interconnected and diverse, the Golden Rule provides a timeless guide for building relationships, resolving conflicts, and creating a more just and equitable society. By embracing the Golden Rule, we not only improve our own lives but also contribute to the well-being of others and to the creation of a more harmonious world.

ᏢᏢᏢ

"Making decisions with our moral compass as our guide ensures that our choices align with our values and principles. It is the path towards ethical living, responsible action, and a life of integrity."

EIGHTEEN

Making Decisions: Applying Our Moral Compass

Making decisions, both large and small, is an inevitable part of life. From choosing what to eat for breakfast to determining our career paths, we are constantly faced with choices that shape our lives and impact the world around us. While some decisions may seem trivial, others have far-reaching consequences, affecting not only ourselves but also our families, communities, and society as a whole. In these moments of choice, our moral compass, a set of internalized values and principles, serves as a guiding light, illuminating the path towards ethical and responsible decision-making.

The moral compass is not a physical object, but rather an internalized framework that helps us navigate complex ethical dilemmas. It is shaped by our upbringing, cultural background, personal experiences, and reflections on life's profound questions. Our moral compass is not static; it evolves and changes as we grow and learn. However, at its core, it is a reflection of our deepest values and beliefs, our understanding of right and wrong, good and bad, just and unjust.

When faced with a decision, our moral compass acts as a filter, helping us to evaluate the available options and choose the path that aligns with our values. It encourages us to consider the potential consequences of our actions, both for ourselves and for others. It prompts us to ask questions such as: "Is this the right thing to do? Will this decision harm anyone? Does it align with my values and principles?"

The process of applying our moral compass to decision-making can be complex and challenging. Often, there are competing values and principles at stake, and the "right" decision may not be immediately clear. In such situations, it is important to engage in a process of thoughtful reflection and deliberation. We may need to gather information, seek advice from trusted individuals, or consult ethical guidelines and resources.

One of the key challenges in applying our moral compass is the presence of biases and cognitive distortions. Our perceptions and judgments can be influenced by a variety of factors, such as our emotions, our past experiences, and the opinions of others. It is important to be aware of these biases and to actively work to mitigate their influence. This can involve seeking out diverse perspectives, challenging our assumptions, and engaging in critical thinking.

Another challenge is the pressure to conform to social norms or expectations. We may feel compelled to make choices that are popular or that align with the views of our peers, even if those choices conflict with our own values. In these situations, it is important to have the courage to stand up for what we believe in, even if it means going against the grain.

Applying our moral compass to decision-making is not a one-time event; it is an ongoing process. As we encounter new situations and challenges, we must continually reassess our values and principles, and refine our understanding of what is right and good. This requires a commitment to self-reflection, a willingness to learn from our mistakes, and a dedication to living a life of integrity.

The benefits of applying our moral compass to decision-making are numerous. It allows us to make choices that are consistent with our values, leading to greater personal fulfillment and a sense of purpose. It also helps us to build stronger relationships, as we are more likely to be trusted and respected by others when we act with integrity and ethical consistency.

In the workplace, applying our moral compass can lead to more ethical and responsible business practices. It can help us to create a more positive and productive work environment, where employees feel valued and empowered. It can also enhance our reputation and credibility, both as individuals and as organizations.

In the broader context of society, applying our moral compass can contribute to the creation of a more just and equitable world. By making choices that are guided by our values, we can promote social justice, environmental sustainability, and human rights. We can also inspire others to do the same, creating a ripple effect of positive change.

The application of our moral compass to decision-making is a complex and ongoing process, but it is essential for living a meaningful and fulfilling life. By taking the time to reflect on our values, to consider the consequences of our actions, and to choose the path that aligns with our deepest beliefs, we can make choices that not only benefit ourselves but also contribute to the well-being of others and to the creation of a better world.

"Community is the fabric of society, the interconnected web of relationships that supports and nourishes us. It is the shared values and ethical principles that bind us together, creating a sense of belonging and purpose."

NINETEEN

COMMUNITY: BUILDING A STRONG MORAL FABRIC

Community, a collective of individuals sharing common interests, values, and a sense of belonging, is an essential pillar of human society. It provides a network of support, fosters a sense of identity, and creates a space for shared experiences and collective action. A strong moral fabric, woven together by shared values, ethical principles, and a commitment to the common good, is the foundation upon which thriving communities are built. This moral fabric is not merely a set of rules or regulations; it is a shared understanding of what is right and good, a collective conscience that guides individual and group behavior.

The importance of community and its moral fabric cannot be overstated. Communities provide a sense of belonging and connection, fulfilling our innate need for social interaction and support. They offer a space for shared experiences, traditions, and cultural practices, fostering a sense of identity and pride. Communities also provide essential services and support systems, such as education, healthcare, and social welfare, that contribute to the well-being of their members.

A strong moral fabric is the glue that holds communities together. Shared values and ethical principles provide a common ground upon which individuals can build trust, cooperation, and mutual respect. When members of a community share a sense of responsibility for each other's well-being, they are more likely to support each other in times of need, to work together to solve problems, and to create a more just and equitable society.

The moral fabric of a community is not static; it evolves and changes over time, shaped by the experiences and values of its members. It is strengthened by active participation in civic life, by open dialogue and debate, and by a commitment to the common good. When individuals engage in their communities, they contribute to the collective conscience, shaping the values and norms that guide behavior.

A strong moral fabric is essential for addressing social challenges and promoting positive change. When communities are united by shared values and a commitment to the common good, they are better equipped to tackle issues such as poverty, inequality, and discrimination. They are more likely to develop innovative solutions, to mobilize resources, and to advocate for policies that benefit all members of the community.

Building a strong moral fabric requires a multi-faceted approach. It starts with individual responsibility, as each member of the community must commit to upholding ethical principles and acting in ways that benefit the greater good. It also requires strong leadership, as community leaders play a crucial role in modeling ethical behavior, promoting dialogue and collaboration, and fostering a sense of shared purpose.

Education also plays a vital role in building a strong moral fabric.

Schools and other educational institutions can teach children and young adults about ethical principles, social responsibility, and the importance of contributing to their communities. By fostering critical thinking, empathy, and a sense of civic engagement, education can empower the next generation to become active and responsible citizens.

The media also has a role to play in shaping the moral fabric of our communities. By highlighting positive stories of individuals and organizations that are making a difference, the media can inspire others to get involved and contribute to the greater good. By promoting ethical journalism and responsible reporting, the media can also help to create a more informed and engaged citizenry.

In today's interconnected world, the concept of community has expanded beyond geographical boundaries. We are increasingly connected to people from all over the world through social media, online forums, and virtual communities. While these online communities offer new opportunities for connection and collaboration, they also present unique challenges in terms of building a strong moral fabric.

Online communities often lack the face-to-face interactions that are essential for building trust and understanding. They can also be more susceptible to the spread of misinformation, hate speech, and other forms of online harassment. It is important for members of online communities to be mindful of the impact of their words and actions, to treat others with respect, and to contribute to a positive and inclusive online environment.

Building a strong moral fabric is an ongoing process that requires the commitment and participation of all members of the community. By embracing shared values, upholding ethical principles, and working together for the common good, we can create communities that are vibrant, resilient, and just. In the words of the Dalai Lama, "If you want others to be happy, practice compassion. If you want to be happy, practice compassion." By cultivating compassion, empathy, and a sense of shared responsibility, we can build a world where everyone can thrive.

ϷϷϷ

"Living a life of purpose and meaning is not a destination but a journey, a continuous process of self-discovery and growth. It is the pursuit of our passions, the use of our talents to serve others, and the connection with something larger than ourselves."

TWENTY

CONCLUSION: LIVING A LIFE OF PURPOSE AND MEANING

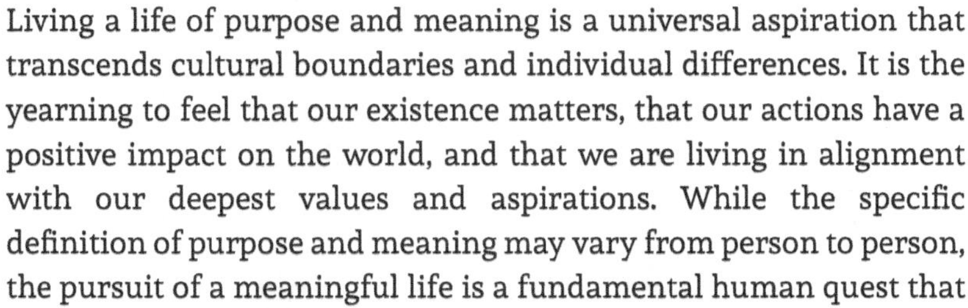

Living a life of purpose and meaning is a universal aspiration that transcends cultural boundaries and individual differences. It is the yearning to feel that our existence matters, that our actions have a positive impact on the world, and that we are living in alignment with our deepest values and aspirations. While the specific definition of purpose and meaning may vary from person to person, the pursuit of a meaningful life is a fundamental human quest that has captivated philosophers, theologians, and everyday individuals for centuries.

At its core, a life of purpose and meaning is one that is lived with intention and direction. It is not simply about accumulating wealth, achieving success, or pursuing pleasure; it is about aligning our actions with our values, using our talents and abilities to contribute to something larger than ourselves, and leaving a positive legacy for future generations. A purposeful life is one that is characterized by passion, engagement, and a deep sense of fulfillment.

The quest for purpose and meaning is not a new phenomenon. Throughout history, individuals have sought to understand their place in the world and to find meaning in their existence. Religions, philosophies, and spiritual traditions have offered various frameworks for understanding purpose and meaning, often emphasizing the importance of connecting with something larger than ourselves, whether it be God, the universe, or humanity as a whole.

In modern times, the search for purpose and meaning has become even more pronounced. As traditional sources of meaning, such as religion and community, have declined in influence, individuals have been left to grapple with existential questions on their own. The rise of individualism and consumerism has also contributed to a sense of disconnection and meaninglessness for many people.

However, the pursuit of purpose and meaning is not a futile endeavor. Research has shown that individuals who have a sense of purpose in their lives tend to be happier, healthier, and more resilient. They are more likely to engage in meaningful activities, to have stronger social connections, and to make a positive impact on the world.

Finding purpose and meaning is not a one-time event; it is an ongoing process. It requires self-reflection, exploration, and a willingness to embrace uncertainty. There is no single formula for finding purpose and meaning, as it is a deeply personal journey that varies from person to person. However, there are some common themes that emerge from the lives of those who have found purpose and meaning.

One common theme is the importance of connecting with something larger than ourselves. This could involve engaging in spiritual or religious practices, volunteering for a cause we care about, or simply spending time in nature. When we connect with something larger than ourselves, we gain a sense of perspective and purpose that transcends our individual lives.

Another common theme is the importance of using our talents and abilities to contribute to the world. Whether it is through our work, our relationships, or our creative endeavors, we find meaning and fulfillment when we use our gifts to make a positive impact on others. This could involve mentoring a young person, starting a business that solves a social problem, or simply being a good friend and neighbor.

The pursuit of purpose and meaning is not always easy. It can be challenging to identify our passions and talents, to overcome obstacles, and to stay motivated in the face of setbacks. However, the rewards are immeasurable. A life of purpose and meaning is a life that is rich, fulfilling, and deeply satisfying. It is a life that is worth living.

In the words of the renowned psychologist Viktor Frankl, "The meaning of life is to give life meaning." By embracing our passions, using our talents to serve others, and connecting with something larger than ourselves, we can create a life that is not only personally fulfilling but also profoundly impactful on the world around us. Through acts of kindness, compassion, and service, we discover purpose and leave a lasting legacy, enriching both our own lives and the lives of others.

❧❧❧

"The moral compass curriculum is a roadmap for ethical living, a guide for navigating life's complexities with integrity, compassion, and purpose. It is an invitation to embrace our shared humanity and to contribute to a more just and equitable world."

TWENTY-ONE
SUMMARY

In an ever-evolving world marked by rapid technological advancements and shifting societal norms, the cultivation of a moral compass stands as an indispensable pillar for navigating life's complexities and fostering a just and compassionate society. This comprehensive exploration has delved into the multifaceted nature of morality, examining its core values, ethical principles, and practical applications.

We began by recognizing the paramount importance of a moral compass, which serves as our guiding light in making decisions that align with our values and principles. It empowers us to navigate ethical dilemmas, build meaningful relationships, and contribute positively to our communities. We explored the fundamental building blocks of morality, namely core values and ethics, which form the bedrock of our moral compass. These deeply held beliefs and guiding principles shape our character, inform our choices, and ultimately determine our actions.

Empathy, the ability to understand and share the feelings of others, emerged as a cornerstone of moral conduct. It allows us to connect with the experiences of others, fostering compassion, understanding, and deeper connections. We examined the virtues of honesty and integrity, which emphasize truthfulness, trustworthiness, and the unwavering adherence to moral and ethical principles. Respect, encompassing both self-respect and respect for others, was recognized as a fundamental value that underpins healthy relationships and social harmony.

We delved into the importance of responsibility, which entails making thoughtful choices and accepting the consequences of our actions. Responsibility empowers us to shape our own lives, contribute to the well-being of our communities, and address global challenges. Fairness, the principle of treating everyone equally and justly, was identified as a crucial component of a just and equitable society. It involves recognizing the inherent worth of every individual and ensuring that everyone has the opportunity to reach their full potential.

Compassion, the feeling of deep sympathy and sorrow for the suffering of others, coupled with a strong desire to alleviate their pain, was highlighted as an essential virtue for a meaningful life. It motivates us to extend kindness, care, and support to those in need, fostering a more just and compassionate world. We explored the virtue of courage, the unwavering resolve to confront fear and adversity in pursuit of a noble goal. Courage empowers us to stand up for what we believe in, to speak out against injustice, and to defend the rights of others.

Perseverance, the unwavering determination to pursue our goals despite obstacles and setbacks, was recognized as a key ingredient for personal growth, achievement, and social progress. It allows us to overcome challenges, learn from our failures, and create a meaningful impact on the world. We delved into the transformative power of gratitude, which involves appreciating the good things in our lives and recognizing the blessings that surround us. Gratitude enhances our well-being, strengthens our relationships, and inspires us to give back to our communities.

Forgiveness, the act of pardoning an offense and releasing negative emotions, was explored as a path towards healing, reconciliation, and inner peace. It liberates us from the burdens of anger and resentment, allowing us to move forward with compassion and understanding. Cooperation, the act of working together for a common purpose, was identified as an essential human behavior that has enabled us to achieve remarkable feats throughout history. It is the driving force behind the creation of complex societies, the development of groundbreaking technologies, and the resolution of global challenges.

Self-discipline, the ability to control our thoughts, emotions, and actions, was recognized as a cornerstone of personal growth, achievement, and moral fortitude. It empowers us to make conscious choices that align with our values and goals, even when faced with temptation or adversity. Humility, the quality of being modest and unassuming in attitude, was identified as a strength that fosters healthy relationships, enhances our ability to learn and grow, and promotes a more grounded and compassionate approach to life.

Generosity, the act of giving and sharing freely, was recognized as a virtue that enriches both the giver and the receiver. It strengthens our bonds with others, fosters trust, and creates a sense of reciprocity. We revisited the Golden Rule, the timeless ethical principle that guides us to treat others as we would like to be treated. It is a call to empathy, encouraging us to put ourselves in the shoes of others and to act in ways that promote understanding, harmony, and mutual respect.

Finally, we explored the importance of building a strong moral fabric within our communities. This involves shared values, ethical principles, and a commitment to the common good. It requires the active participation of all members of the community, as well as strong leadership, education, and responsible media.

In conclusion, the cultivation of a moral compass is an ongoing journey, one that requires self-reflection, introspection, and a willingness to learn and grow. By embracing the values and principles discussed in this exploration, we can make choices that are not only beneficial for ourselves but also contribute to the well-being of others and to the creation of a more just, equitable, and compassionate world.

As we navigate the complexities of the 21st century, the importance of a moral compass cannot be overstated. It is the compass that guides us through turbulent waters, the anchor that keeps us grounded in our values, and the beacon that illuminates the path towards a more meaningful and fulfilling life.

ᐅᐅᐅ

Citation And References

This book represents the culmination of extensive research and meticulous analysis, incorporating a diverse range of sources, including numerous books, scholarly studies, and personal experiences. Additionally, I have scoured various websites to gather relevant information and data essential for the compilation of this work. I have taken every precaution to ensure the accuracy of the information presented and have diligently cited all sources to acknowledge their contributions.

Despite these efforts, the possibility of inadvertent errors remains. I deeply value the insights of my readers and appreciate any feedback that can help identify and rectify such inaccuracies. I encourage you to bring any discrepancies to my attention.

Your feedback is not only welcome but crucial, as it will aid in correcting current editions and enhancing the content of future ones. I am committed to maintaining the highest standards of accuracy and reliability in my work and thank you for your support and understanding.

Additionally, I firmly uphold the principle of freedom of speech and expression as guaranteed under Article 19(1)(a) of the Constitution of India, and I respect the diverse viewpoints and expressions of all readers.

❦❦❦

Other Books Of The Author

1. Empowering Minds: A Journey into Women's Self-Discovery and Power
2. The Dynamics of Motivation: Catalyzing Thought into Action
3. Meditation and Mental Well Being: The Path to Inner Peace and Clarity
4. The Psychology of Child Education: Nurturing Future Generations
5. Ethical Enlightenment: A Modern Guide to Living with Integrity
6. Voices of Empowerment: Stories of Women Rising Against Odds
7. Social Psychology in Everyday Life: Understanding Human Connections
8. The Essence of Motivational Speaking: Inspiring Change in Others
9. Balancing Acts: Women, Work, and the Will to Lead
10. Guiding with Grace: Raising Children with Compassion and Awareness
11. The Power of Positive Aging: Embracing Life After Fifty
12. Building Resilient Communities: Social Work in Action
13. The Ethical Educator: Principles for Teaching and Learning
14. From Insight to Impact: Social Psychology for a Better World
15. The Ethics of Empathy: A Guide to Ethical Living
16. The Science of Empowering the Self: Navigating Life's Challenges with Psychological Wisdom
17. The Mindful Conscious Leader: Meditation Techniques for Modern Management
18. Pioneering Spirit: Women's Pathways to Leadership and Empowerment
19. Feeling to Healing: The Role of Emotional Intelligence in Child Development
20. Transformative Talks and Words of Inspiration: Insights into Motivational Oratory

21. Green Ethics: A Path to Sustainable Living
22. Spiritual Integrity: Navigating Life with Moral Compassion
23. Clean Living, Clean Society: The Ethics of Cleanliness
24. Patriotic Spirits: Building a Nation on Positive Attitudes
25. Innovative Integrity & Vibrant Visions: The Ethical and Entrepreneurial Spirit of Gujarat
26. Youthful Visions, Endless Possibilities: Inspiring Ethics and Motivation in Children
27. Living Your Legacy: How to Motivate Others by Living Your Values
28. Secret of Healing Conversations: Ethical Practices in Counselling and Therapy
29. Creative Kindness: Crafting a Life of Compassion and Creativity
30. The Power of Appreciation: How Gratitude Can Transform Your Relationships
31. Bhagavad-Gita: Messages
32. Science of Art: The New Frontier of Fashion Modernism
33. Vivekananda's Virtues: A Blueprint for Modern Living
34. Empower Her: Navigating the Path to Women's Entrepreneurship
35. The Boundless Classroom: Innovations in Global Education
36. The Language of Leadership: Communicating with Authenticity and Impact
37. The Warrior's Mantra: Deciphering the Hanuman Chalisa
38. Echoes of Empathy: Transformative Stories of Social Service
39. Artful Living: Cultivating Creativity in Your Daily Routine
40. Finding Your Why: Discovering Your Passions and Charting Your Course
41. The Role of Social Media in Shaping Self-Esteem and Interpersonal Relationships among Adolescents
42. Karma's Tapestry: Weaving a Life of Selfless Service
43. Altruistic Alchemy: Transforming Lives Through Giving
44. The Blueprint of Pro-Activeness and Productivity: Crafting Habits for Success
45. The Simplicity with Grounded Wisdom: Embracing Authenticity

in a Complex World

46. Secret of Solopreneur's Odyssey: Navigating the Path to Self-Employment
47. Exploring Tapestry of Peace: Global Perspectives on Harmony
48. The Art and Actions of Connection: Mastering Communication for Impact
49. She Governs and at the Helm: Strategies for Political Empowerment
50. Rising Above and Rising with Grace: A Woman's Roadmap to Career Mastery
51. The Effect of Networking & Connectedness: Building Strategic Alliances for Women
52. Beyond his Barriers: Women Thriving in Male-Dominated Fields
53. Secret of Inner Compass: Navigating Life with Intuition
54. Creative & Pro-Active Muses: A Celebration of Women in the Arts
55. Unburdened: The Art of Releasing the Past
56. Amplified Voices: Speeches of Women that Astonished the World
57. Secret of Manifesting Dreams: A Woman's Guide to Intentional Living
58. Ethics and Value Based Education: Reimagining Japan's School System
59. The Moral Compass Curriculum: A Holistic Approach
60. Tech with Heart: Integrating Ethics into Digital Learning
61. Honoring Virtue: Recognizing Ethical Excellence in Education
62. Raising Good Humans: A Guide to Character Development
63. The Spark Within: Nurturing Creativity in Children
64. The Teenager Whisperer: Navigating Adolescence with Grace
65. Igniting a Passion for Learning: Inspiring Lifelong Curiosity
66. The Habit Lab: Cultivating Positive Behaviors in Children
67. Seeds of Empathy: Fostering Compassion in Young Hearts
68. The Reading Revolution: Inspiring a Love of Books in Children
69. The Learning Brain: Unlocking the Secrets of Student Success
70. Teaching for All: Differentiated Instruction Strategies
71. The Time Alchemist: Mastering Time Management for Peak Performance

Bhajan
101. Pilgrimage of the Soul: Spiritual Journeys in India

❦❦❦

Contact

Dr. Minakshi Bansal
Social Activist
Ahmedabad, Gujarat, Bharat
minakshiindiag20@yahoo.com

❥❥❥

|| LOKAHA SAMASTHAHA SUKHINO BHAVANTU ||